SWING TRAD

I0037139

A Beginner's Guide to Making
Money with Trend Following

BOOK DESCRIPTION

Financial markets are some of the best markets to trade in today. Trading in equities (stocks) is among the most lucrative businesses available to you today. It does not matter whether you are a one-person small-scale trader or a giant corporation. This multitrillion-dollar pie is a great opportunity.

This book, 'A Beginners Guide to Making Money With Trend Following' is specifically written for you – the beginner. It starts with a basic introductory approach that enables you to understand the key concepts of Swing trading, a unique strategy of trading in financial securities.

Life without risk is non-existent. Every business has its own risk. The risk is the cost of doing business. What differentiates a shrewd trader from an ordinary trader is the ability to know, understand and appreciate risk. It is upon this knowledge, understanding and appreciation that a trader can be able to plan for it, establish safety mechanism and establish how much he/she is willing to risk to maximize profits. This book provides you with information on various risks associated with trend following and the best strategies to manage them.

Every decision you make and action you take is based on certain parameters. These parameters have both the lower limit and the upper limit. When a certain anticipated event causes the equity to break the limits, a decision has to be made and an action was taken. There must be triggers, signals or indicators that notify you that the limits have been broken. In Swing trading, breaking the limits is what is commonly referred to as 'breakouts'. Breakouts are extremely significant as they enable you to decide to buy or sell. This book guides you on how to establish limits, detect breakouts and maximize opportunities for making money.

Inevitably, every business starts somewhere. Companies that decide to go public, that is, being listed on the securities market must make an IPO. An IPO is an acronym for Initial Public Offering. Naturally, and traditionally, IPOs attract significant interest. This brings a lot of speculation and price swings. This is a rare opportunity for a swing trader to make a big profit. You too can make a big profit out of IPO. In this book, we endear to help you succeed.

They say one man's meat is another man's poison. This is so true with securities markets. When one decides to enter the market, another one decides to leave. When one makes a sell decision, another one makes a buy decision. Similarly, when a bull is climbing up a hill, a bear is descending down. Bears and Bulls, bearish and bullish aptly describe players in the securities market and their respective habits. Are you are a bear or a bull? We will let you know.

Announcements are crucial when it comes to securities markets. They provide information that helps to shape decisions. An earnings announcement is one such crucial piece of information that leads certain market behaviors and triggers ripples that bring about swings. As a swing trader, you must keep your ears on the ground. How does an earning announcement affect your position? In this guide, it is our duty to let you know.

Enjoy reading!

GIFT INCLUDED

If you are an entrepreneur, an aspiring entrepreneur, someone who is trying to create additional income stream or even someone who just loves self-improvement books; then you need to read my recommendations for top 10 business books ever. These books read by me have changed my life for the better.

<u>Top 10 Business Books</u>

ABOUT THE AUTHOR

George Pain is an entrepreneur, author and business consultant. He specializes in setting up online businesses from scratch, investment income strategies and global mobility solutions. He has successfully built several businesses from the ground up and is excited to share his knowledge with you. Here is a list of his books.

Books of George Pain

DISCLAIMER

CONTENTS

INTRODUCTION

Trading is all about making a profit. In a multitrillion-dollar market like the securities markets, the potential for serious profits is real. However, few are missing these huge potential profits simply due to lack of information and expertise.

In this guide, we not only introduce you to a unique kind of trading – swing trading, but also how to profit from it. An experienced trader is a one who has mastered the history of his business and can easily use such historical data to predict the future. Luckily, for securities markets, this information is readily available. There are also many tools that can enable you to forecast and make projections basing on the trend – a historical journey of a given stock. By following the trend, you can determine when to buy a stock and when to sell at a profit. Trend following is one of the best ways to make money while trading securities. Information provided in this book is aimed at exactly this – helping you make money through trend following.

Keep reading!

WHAT IS SWING TRADING?

Trading in equity stocks is one of the easiest businesses to do. Most markets have online platforms that make it easy for you to trade online at your own convenience. Many people enter stock markets as investors rather than traders. Investing is long-term with the aim making capital gains. However, you can still enter equity stock markets not as an investor but as a trader.

Swing trading is one the most popular trading activities on the financial securities markets.

What is a swing?

A swing is a significant fluctuation in the value of an asset or account.

What is swing trading?

Swing trading is a speculative activity in securities market where a tradable asset is held for several days with an aim of profiting in a swing.

Why you need to differentiate between swing trading and investing

A big mistake that new entrants to securities market make is the failure to distinguish between trading and investing. In trading, your desire is to maximize profit. In investing, your desire is to maximize wealth. Thus, although your ultimate aim could be becoming wealthy, trading and investing are two distinct approaches.

Trading is short-term and its focus is on the price differential. Your aim is to maximize the net positive difference between your purchase price (cost) and selling price (revenue). The bigger the net positive difference the bigger is the profit. If you keep on accumulating these profits, you end up building your wealth.

Investing is long-term. In investing, you seek a security whose fundamental value will keep rising. Thus, you are acquiring a capital asset (equity), as opposed to a revenue asset (stock).

While trading, your focus is more on price movement and thus you use technical analysis, in investing, the focus is more on intrinsic value and thus you use fundamental analysis.

If you approach swing trading with an investor's mindset, you are likely not going to maximize profit. You must approach swing trading with a trader's mindset. An investor's mindset may cause you to cling to a stock while you ought to have sold it, thus losing on revenue. A trader has no inherent interest in clinging to a stock except to maximize profit.

What are the pros and cons of swing trading?

Swing trading, like any other engagement, has its own pros and cons.

Pros

1. Higher profit potential - Compared to day trading, swing trading has relatively higher profit potential
2. Time convenience – Unlike day trading where you must keep an eye on the market, swing trading consumes less time. This allows you to carry it out on a part-time basis while engaging in other income generating activities.
3. Greater risk/reward ratio – Swings have higher potential to achieve your profit target than day trading. The risk/reward ratio of between 1:3 and 1:10 is common.
4. Les strain – Besides saving on time, swing trading is less stressful as your adrenalin does not have to keep oscillating with minor price blips occasioned with day trading. Swing trading has the potential for larger price blips that are less likely to challenge your protected stop price.

Cons

1. Bigger protective stop orders – Relative to day trading, the protective stop orders are generally bigger. This means that you have a bigger portfolio exposed to risk than with

day trading. That means you need better risk management to safeguard your portfolio.

2. Congestion – Sometimes the market can be congested characterized by violent swings in both directions. This can stop you out repeatedly thus causing you voluminous losses.

3. Uncontrolled appetite – Due to it being time-friendly and low-strain, one may be tempted to enter into several markets thus exposing more portfolios to risk. This is not a market problem but a habitual problem that you can deal with.

What is the best Swing Trading Strategy?

In simplest terms, swing-trading strategies are those strategies that let you:

- Buy on the downswing when price is just about to turn up
- Sell on the upswing when the price is just about to turn down.

Essentially, it is all about buying at the bottom and selling at the top.

Essential building blocks to swing trading strategy

- Establishing a trend
- Detecting retracements to a trend
- Entering the trend at the most optimal price
- Risking less for more
- Hitting quick profit gains

A basic swing trading strategy

The following is a basic swing strategy that you can advance on through practice and experience:

- Enter the trend when price surpasses the previous swing high (concludes above the new high)
- Set your stop-loss just below or at the previous swing low
- Scale up the stop-loss upon every new swing low

Swing trading steps

The following are basic steps required to implement a swing strategy:

1. Carry out scanning to identify stocks to trade – a proper stock trading app has filter options that allow you to carry out effective scanning.
2. Use chart patterns to identify high probability chart setups.
3. Establish an entry point based on a good risk/reward ratio

4. Establish an exit point based on a position that will maximize profits

Bear vs. Bull

In Swing trading and trading in equities and securities in general, it is important to know the difference between Bear and Bull and thus be able to determine as to whether you are a going to hold a bear position or a bull position.

What is a bear?

A bear is an investor with a pessimistic mindset regarding a given stock and thus prefers reaping from its downward trend.

Bear behavior

A bear utilizes techniques that enable him to make profits when the market falls, with a risk of making losses when the market rises. One of the most common techniques used by bears is short selling. Short selling involves buying low and selling high, but in reverse order. That is, selling first and then buying later, in the hope that price has declined.

Short selling becomes profitable with the act of borrowing shares for sale rather than buying to sell.

How does a bear make a profit?

A bear borrows a certain volume of stock from a broker in the hope that their price will go down. He then sells them afterward and returns the same volume of stock to the broker when the prices are down. This way, he makes a profit from the difference. For example, buy 100 shares worth $1 from a broker. Sell them at probably $0.9 each (amounting to $90). When the value of drops to $0.4 buy back 100 shares (amounting to $40) and return to the brokers. The broker will get back the exact number of shares that you borrowed. However, you will have made a profit of $50 (that is, $90 - $40 = $50).

What is a bull?

A bull is an investor with an optimistic mindset regarding a given stock/stock market and thus prefers reaping from an upward trend (that is, buying low and selling high). A bull focuses on the upward trend.

Bull Markets vs. Bear Markets

A bull market is characterized by positive sentiments and optimism. This creates demand for stocks, which cause prices to go on an upward trend.

On the other hand, a bear market is characterized by negative sentiments and pessimism. This causes prices to go a general trend of decline.

RISKS OF TREND FOLLOWING

Any investment involves risks. In fact, investment is about risk to benefit from its reward. Without risk, you cannot make an investment. Even the most secure investment has an apparent risk.

Swing trading also involves risks of its own. How you perceive and treat risks depends on your mindset. Your mindset determines your level of risk tolerance.

Risk tolerance simply refers to the level of risk, which an investor is willing to take in carrying out a given investment decisions.

Before we dwell further on the risks of trend following, let us understand the different kinds of risk mindsets;

- **Risk-averse** – This mindset avoids risk as much as it can. A risk-averse mindset will invest more in safe hedges. It pays more attention to safety than returns. It loves stability and hates swings. A risk-averse mindset exhibits low levels of risk tolerance.
- **Risk taker** – This mindset appreciates risks and believes in the philosophy that 'the higher the risk, the higher the reward'. A risk taker focuses on higher rewards and

appreciates huge swings. A risk taker exhibits high levels of risk tolerance.

- **Risk-neutral** – This mindset is neither risk-averse nor risk taker. It is more balanced. It considers the importance of risk as the sacrifice necessary to invest but does not assume it. A risk neutral mindset looks for an equilibrium point where risk and reward balance out. However, such a point is more idealistic than reality. A risk neutral considers other factors as more important than risk and thus, has less consideration towards risks. For example, a risk-neutral mindset will consider how reputable a company is rather than how volatile its stocks are in the market. A risk neutral mindset exhibits moderate levels of risk tolerance.

From the foregoing, you can realize that swing trading is not for the risk-averse. Swing trading favors the risk takers.

Risk tolerance vs. Risk capacity

While risk tolerance refers to a measure of willingness to absorb risk, risk capacity refers to your ability to tolerate risk. Thus, tolerance is qualitative in nature while capacity is quantitative in nature. While risk tolerance is more rigid, risk capacity is very flexible. Risk capacity depends on your very own unique financial situation. If your financial situation improves, then, you have more portfolios to risk. On the other hand, if your financial situation contracts, you have a smaller portfolio to risk.

Risk strategy

Every risk strategy is based on one's risk tolerance. Risk strategy encompasses the following steps:

1. Determine your own investment time horizon – How urgent or soon you need your money back will determine your investment horizon. This could be days, weeks, months or years. Stocks are rather volatile in the short-term than in the long-term. Thus, if you have low-risk tolerance levels, you would wish to invest more conservatively in the short-term and more liberally in the long-term.

2. Consider alternative income streams – Your dependency on one income stream increases your vulnerability towards it. Thus, if stock trading is your primary source of income, then, you are more vulnerable. Thus, you would be more cautious about risks. However, if you have a regular paying job or other regular incomes such as rental income, then, you would be more willing to take higher risks in stock trading. This will also influence your investment time horizon because, if you solely depend on

stock trading income, then, you would need a significant portfolio that produces income flows in the short-term to meet your daily consumption needs.

3. Establish your persistence level – Stocks can go weak before rallying back stronger. If you are incapable of persisting longer, probably due to pressing cash needs that require you to dispose of your stake, then, you will not last long enough to reap their strong position.

4. Match your asset allocation with your risk tolerance – Your asset allocation (cash) towards your stock portfolio should match what you consider safe enough to risk without disrupting your everyday income needs.

Stock risk management tools and techniques

Several tools and techniques that you can employ in stock risk management. These tools and techniques include:

1. Stop Loss Limit Order

2. Options

Stop Loss Limit Order

This is an order placed with a broker which combines the benefits of a stop order and limit order. This order will automatically execute at a specified price or better after a specified price has been reached.

Options

There are two main types of options:

- Call option – This is an instrument that grants the buyer right, with no obligation attached, to purchase a given stock at a particular price within a defined period.

- Put option – This is an instrument that grants the seller the right, with no obligation attached, to sell a certain number of a given stock at a particular price within a defined period.

Tips and hacks on risk management:

1. Set stop-loss order

2. Set risk/reward ratio

3. Carry out position sizing

What is a trend?

Well, literary, almost everyone knows what a trend is. The same meaning applies to financial securities. However, we can expand it a bit further in the context of financial securities.

A trend is simply the general direction of the price of a stock or of a stock market.

Types of trends

There are several types of trends. However, they can be classified based on two broad factors:

- Direction
- Time

Trends based on direction

Based on direction, we do have two types of trends:

1. Uptrend – This is characterized by a series of higher highs and retracements that create lower lows
2. Downtrend – This is characterized by a series of lower lows and retracements that create lower highs

Trends based on duration

This refers to how long a trend lasts in its direction. Thus, we have three main types:

1. Primary trends – Also referred to as major trends. They last from several months to years.

2. Secondary trends – These are embedded within a primary trend and lasts from several weeks to a few months
3. Short-term trends – These last from several days to a few weeks.

How to identify a trend

To identify a trend, begin with a daily chart interval. If there is no clear trend, switch to a higher time frame. When observing a possible trend, do not forget that trends experience periods of corrections. They also experience sideways trends commonly known as consolidation or ranging. While a shorter timeframe may show sideways, a longer time frame may smoothen them out.

What creates a trend?

Trends are normally formed by participants' reactions due to behavioral biases. The following are some of these behavioral biases:

- Herding – This is the tendency of many players jumping on a bandwagon once a trend appears to be cited, thus elongating it.
- Confirmation bias – Human nature is such that it seeks views, opinions, and information that support their biased position and beliefs. This is commonly witnesses by investors buying stocks that have recently higher earnings

and selling those that have recently shown lower earnings, thus facilitating upward or downward trend, respectively.

- Risk tolerance bias – If most investors have the same level of risk tolerance, then, they are more likely going to react the same way to market information thus pushing forward a trend.

What is trend following?

Trend following is a trade (or investment) strategy characterized by seeking to take advantage of short, medium and long-term moves in various markets. In this regard, trend followers do not aim to forecast specific price levels. They simply jump onto a trend and seek to benefit from price differentials along it.

Trend followers enter the market after a trend properly establishes itself on the hope that it will persist along its path for a significantly long time.

Why trend following?

The following are key reasons why trend following helps:

- To plan ahead – A trend moves in a certain direction. When you know the general trend, you can easily understand the prevailing market and plan appropriately.
- To improve predictability – A trend helps one to set price targets and consequently profit targets.
- To reduce risk – Knowledge helps you avoid risks. A trend helps you to know which securities are doing well in the market and which ones are not. This way, you can reduce your risk by avoiding those that are not doing well.
- To maximize possible opportunities – A trend helps you identify similar securities that you can invest in.
- To determine entry and exit points – Knowing when to enter a market and when to exit are crucial. Entering prematurely means your money is exposed to more risk. Exiting prematurely means you miss out on profit opportunities. Entering late means that you will have to buy stocks at a higher price. Exiting late means that you risk your profit being chewed up by falling prices.

What are the benefits of trend following?

The following are some of the benefits of trend following:

- High returns – Trend following offers higher returns compared to scalping and day trading.
- Lower risk - Trend following offers lower risk compared to scalping and day trading.

- Time value of money – Unlike investing, swing trading helps you to net value sooner than later.
- Less cost of forecasting – Trend followers need not sweat hard, they only need to identify a trend, set profit target and ride on it to the target.
- No need for tons of information – You need not stress and overload yourself with stories and gossip milling around in financial news outlets
- Can work passively – You do not need to spend many hours every day sitting behind your computer screen to monitor the market every day. Once you identify your trend and set profit target, all you need is to wait.
- Clear-cut strategy – Trend following is about opportunity taking as opposed to opportunity making. Just ride on the trend's back.
- Straightforward – You do not need to learn tons of indicators and dozens of theorems. You can easily narrow down to your core concepts.
- No information overload – Simple concepts, basic strategies are all you need.
- No brand allegiance – You are not tethered to any brand or favorite stock. It is all about trends.

- A blessed unrest – Chaos, uncertainties, surprise events – things that most avoid, are all that you need to reap big from swings.

What are the best trend indicators?

There are two main types of technical indicators:

1. Trending indicators – These indicators help to establish a trend so that you can know the general direction of a given stock or market.
2. Momentum indicators – These indicators show price movements. More so, how fast prices are moving.

What are the risks of trend following?

- Overnight risk – This is a risk characterized by a shift in security prices as the day moves to the next.
- Taking profits too early – This is a risk of setting up profit target too low on a trend so that you take profits before the trend grows to higher levels. In this case, you lose out on further profits.
- Late exits – This is a risk which you lose out on profit due to setting your profit target too high such that the trend reverses before reaching your target.
- High commissions – The shorter the trading period, the higher the commission. For example, commission on day trading is usually higher than the commission on swing

trading. On the other hand, long-term investments have lower commission than swing trading.

Trend following – factors to consider

While you prepare yourself to venture into the trend following business, note the following factors that you ought to keep in your mind:

- Price – Trend following is about price. This is your primary concern. You only need to watch what the current price is to know what the market is doing. Too many predictions are not necessary.
- Money management – Once a trend establishes, you ride on it. What is important is not timing but how much to trade over the course of the trend.
- Risk control – The basic rule is cut down on your losses. The main objective is to preserve capital until a more positive trend establishes. Thus, during periods of high market volatility, trading size is reduced. Similarly, during losing periods, the position is reduced, and trade size cut back.
- Diversification – It is necessary to diversify into several manageable markets to spread risks.

- Rules – Price and timing are key at all times. Thus, trend following ought to be systematic.

Trend following indicators

Indicators are a great way to simplify price information. They also provide trend trade signals and warn of reversals.

Indicators are applicable to all time frames. They can also be customized to suit each trader's unique needs and preferences.

Types of trend following indicators:

- Moving averages – These smoothen out price data thus forming a one moving line which represents price averages over a relevant range (time duration). The choice of moving average depends on trading time frame. Trend enthusiasts prefer a 50-day, 100-day, and 200-day moving averages. There are a number of ways to interpret moving averages. The first way is to observe the angular inclination of the moving average. In case it is predominantly moving laterally for a long duration, then there is no price trend. Ranging is taking place. If it is inclined downwards, a downtrend is underway. If it inclined upwards, an upward trend is happening. The second is the crossovers. Crossovers occur when a 50-day line crosses above a 200-day line when both are plotted against each other on the same chart. A buy indicator happens when the price cuts above a moving average while a sell indicator is identified when price cuts below a moving average.

- MACD – This is an acronym for Moving Average Convergence Divergence. This is momentum indicator used in trend following. It is based on fluctuations below or above 0. If the lines are over 0 for a persistent duration, then, there is a likely upward trend. On the other hand, if the lines are lower than zero for a persistent duration, then, there is likely downward trend. A potential sell signal happens when MACD crosses below 0. Potential buy signals occur when MACD soars above 0. A MACD comprises a pair of lines: a slow one and a fast one. A sell decision happens when the fast line cuts through and under the slow line. On the other hand, a buy decision occurs when the fast one cuts through and over the slow one. Combining MACD with other indicators makes the signal interpretations more clear.

- RSI – This is an acronym for Relative Strength Index. Like MACD, this is another oscillator. However, since its movement happens between 0 and 100, its information is a bit different from that of MACD. When RSI is above 70, the price is overbought – and thus due for a correction. When the price reaches 70 and beyond for sustained periods, that indicates an uptrend. On the other hand, if the indicator is lower than 30, the price is oversold – and thus due to a bounce. When price rests at 30 or lowers persistently for long, it indicates a downtrend. A buy indicator happens when the indicator goes lower than 50 and bounces back over it. This simply indicates that a pullback price has taken place and the investor is purchasing when the pullback is apparently closed (ended) with the trend on recovery. 50 is considered ideal since RSI hardly hit 30 in a rising trend unless signifying a likely reversal. A short-trade indicator happens on a downtrend and RSI goes over 50 and subsequently rescinds lower than the indicator.

- OBV– This is an acronym for On Balance Volume. The volume-based indicator is important, especially in trend following. OBV grabs huge volumes data and to bring out a single-line indicator. OBV measures cumulative selling/buying pressure by summing up the volume on gaining days and minus from it volume on losing days. A falling price should be complemented by a falling OBV while a rising price should be accompanied by a rising OBV. This way, a trend is confirmed.

BREAKOUTS

Everything has its own limits. If you plan to succeed, you must be able to establish the operational limits within which to perform. This same concept applies to stock trading and even more so, to swing trading. Exploding outside these limits will alert you that you need to make a critical decision or take a critical action. Exploding this limit is what is generally known as a breakout. However, in the stock trading parlance, this has its own unique meaning.

What is a breakout?

A breakout is simply a movement of price outside the set price range characterized by an increase in volume. This range is demarcated by the support and resistance levels.

Characteristically, a long position is entered after the stock price goes beyond the resistance level. Alternatively, a short position is entered after the stock price hits beyond the support level.

Volatility goes up when a stock breaks out of the support or resistance level. After the breakout, the price trend establishes in the breakout direction. Normally, this breakout initiates a startup point for major price trends. Thus, breakouts are crucial indicators for trading strategy as they mark the beginning of larger price swings with potentially higher profit margins.

What is breakout trading?

Breakout trading is a custom of purchasing securities when they break down below a previous support level or breakup above a previous resistance level.

What are the key breakout indicators?

For successful breakout trading, the market should be either up trending or range-bound, with price action being as close as possible to the upper end of that range. Indicators help one to confirm a breakout and predict its strength.

The following are key breakout indicators:

- MACD (Moving Average Convergence/Divergence) – MACD is the most commonly used indicator of financial activities. This is because it is simple yet more dependable. It can also be analyzed by use of a histogram template. When a histogram increases in size, it signifies a rise in momentum. When prices and indicators under consideration move in the opposite direction, this sparks off divergences. This enables one to spot a reversal. Being an indicator of momentum, MACD shows movement when a market trend is triggered. This feature enables one to identify a trend that can potentially close abruptly thought it is continuing at the current moment.

- RSI (Relative Strength Indicator) – This indicator is extremely useful to confirm reversal breakouts. It creates divergences, spotting which in time can aid in predicting likely trend reversals. RSI is a great indicator in helping you establish how long a trend has been oversold or overbought. If RSI is 30 or goes below, the market is said to be oversold. On the other hand, if it is over 70, the market is said to be overbought.
- The volume Indicator – Volume indicators such as Volume Weighted Moving Average (VWMA) helps in supporting non-trending indicators to bring more clarity. They help in assessing trend health.

What is the best swing trading breakout strategy?

This is a methodology that allows a trader to find an entry point into a trade and take a position at the formative point of a trend.

The following are key elements of a breakout strategy:

1. Breakout Catalyst

This strategy is anchored on movements in price triggered by an external event (catalyst). In this case, the catalyst is an event that results in a great impact on the market. For example, outcomes of US Presidential election, Brexit, the commodities run, etc. Such events are generally unpredictable and thus their announcements become the focus of quick reflections on the prevailing market. This mostly considered by institutional investors who decide to either accumulate or offload a sizeable volume of securities. These investors base their decision on their assessment of the socio-economic impact of the catalyst.

Swing traders establish and affirm a catalyst that can push huge quantities of trade beyond the resistance and resultant breakout. Uptrends with soaring quantities typically signify a strong breakout. Breakout volumes that expand beyond recent market activities confirm the strength of the trend.

Consolidation breakouts can be identified when complemented by prior uptrend and sideways behaviors characterized by high resistance. Volumes are ascertained on an upward trend at the point the price concludes (closes) beyond previous top-most swing spot on a soaring quantity. It is considered as high probability for persistence when the closure takes place above the previous top-most swing spot on a declined quantity.

In case an investor buys a pullback after the breakout (green) and prior to the security breakout at the previous swing spot, a trader may choose to keep the position depending on the proven likelihood of a persisting uptrend. Upon subsequent pullbacks, the investor may choose to trade while basing on breakout away from the previous top-most swing spot depending on the increased quantities.

Catalysts can be bankruptcies, mergers, acquisitions, drastic changes in earnings (such as profit warning) and such other critical financial announcements can serve as catalysts.

To successfully profit on a catalyst breakout an investor ought to be able to understand the likely consequence of the respective catalyst.

2. Donchian Breakouts

This indicator shows the stocks resistance and support and hence helps to establish volatility and thus ascertain short and long positions. It is an indicator based on moving average.

Daily charts can be used to determine channel breakouts and thus find out volatile markets recently transformed into less volatile over the trading period ranging from 1 to two weeks.

3. Gap Filling

A gap results from a stock opening higher than it closed previously. The difference between the opening higher price and the previous closing price represents its value.

As prices go down, the stock is considered to have undergone a 'gapped down'. On the other hand, as prices rise, the stock is considered to have undergone a 'gapped up'.

Types of Gaps

There are three basic types of gaps:

- The breakaway gap – This is a gap that happens at the end of a price pattern and indicates the beginning of a new trend.
- Continuation gap – This occurs in the middle of a price pattern and indicates a rush of sellers or buyers who share a common belief in the respective stock's future direction
- Common gap – This cannot be placed in a price pattern. It simply indicates an area where the price has gapped.
- Exhaustion gap – This happens at the end of a price pattern and indicates a final attempt to high new lows or highs

Earnings announcements are usually common drivers of gaps. This information must be price sensitive. Typically, gaps close when swing traders place stops at or below the point the gap was created.

To mitigate gap risks, swing traders avoid holding prior to company earnings, sound diversification and position-sizing, and higher reward-to-risk ration.

Swing traders make a profit by purchasing oversold gap fill setups. Trade risk is likely to rise in relation to a gap beyond expected entry prices and gap past stop loss orders. Gaps could also occur across the stop loss order, thus triggering the order to the opening stock price.

To Fill or Not to Fill

When a trader claims that a gap has been 'filled', that means that the price has rescinded to the original pre-gap level. When gaps are filled the very same day of their occurrence, this is known as fading.

4. Dead Cat Bounce

This is a short recovery from a persistent downward trend followed by a continuation of a downward trend.

This event is characterized by a sharp dramatic drop in prices, a V-shaped bounce back and a resumption of decline at relatively moderate rates. This starts with a price gap, followed by a trend low and then a bounce followed by a post-bounce decline and lastly a second bounce.

This even indicates voluminous selling, a broken up uptrend, and a subsequent declining process.

When the price breaks out below the price where the dead cat bounce occurred, that signals swing traders to trade with a downtrend. On the downward breakout point, sell the stock short.

Breakout trading steps

The following key steps can greatly guide you:

1. Identify the candidate – Detect securities with established bold resistance or support levels and monitor them. Keep in mind that the bolder the resistance or support level, the juicier the outcome.
2. Relax as you watch out breakout – After identification do not make a quick jump into trading. This could be premature. Patiently wait for the security price to breakout. To be certain that the breakout stays, on the very same day that the security price goes beyond its resistance

or support level, wait up to near the close of business hours to transact.

3. Set a realistic objective – It is important to set your target objectives. This will guide on the exit point upon which to reap your profits. Computing the range between resistance and support (more so, when trading patterns) or computing, on average, a move made by the stock can help you set target objectives.

4. Let the security Retest – After breaking the resistance level, the old support level becomes the new resistance level. In most circumstances, the security will retry (retest) the previous level it had broken within the first few days.

5. Appreciate when your pattern/trade has failed – A pattern or breakout fails when the security unsuccessful attempt to retry a previous resistance or support level and it bounces back via it. At this point, it is prudent you take your losses instead of gambling with them.

6. Exit towards the market conclusion (close) – At the start of the market, it is hard to establish if prices will stay at a given level. This is the key reason why you may need to wait until almost to the close of the market to exit a losing (bad) trade. In case the stock has stayed outside a pre-

established resistance or support level toward the market conclusion, the moment is ripe to conclude the position and go on to the subsequent.

7. Make a targeted exit – In case you are successfully exiting (without a loss), that means you are still in the trade. Just stay put up to the point when the security price attains its target objective.

IDENTIFYING HIGH REWARD AND LOW-RISK OPPORTUNITIES

Every trader desires to maximize returns. Yet, swing trading relies on stock volatility to make a gain. This means that risk is an inevitable factor. Generally, investments with high risks have the potential to yield higher returns and vice versa. However, there exist those unique opportunities, only available for the information-savvy conscious few, where high reward can be achieved from a low-risk opportunity. To identify such opportunity requires a deliberate and sustained consciousness. This requires you to have a good strategy.

A swing trading strategy to find low-risk profitable trades with price action and trends

The risk is an important component of trade and investment, more so, securities. You cannot completely eliminate risks when it comes to securities, but you can minimize them as much as possible or even develop some mechanism to offset them.

However, it is fundamental to note that how you deal with risk depends on your trading/investment strategy. Thus, it all starts at the strategic level.

The following are necessary building blocks for a reasonable swing trading strategy for high reward low-risk opportunities:

- Establishing a trend
- Ascertaining retracements to the trend
- Entering the trend at the best price possible
- Risking a smaller amount relative to profit potential
- Getting out quickly once you hit your profit target.

What you need to know to master swing trading strategy in order to identify high reward, low-risk opportunities

- Hone your skills in identifying trends
- Master how support and resistance work
- Grasp how to use Fibonacci retracement tool
- Be able to identify and interpret price action candlestick patterns
- Understanding your average holding lifespan (from few days to several weeks)
- Practice patience required for waiting for the right conditions in order to enter a trade
- Know and cultivate the right mindset required for swing trading

PROFITS FROM IPOs

Just to remind ourselves, IPO is an acronym for Initial Public Offering. In most cases, it is common for new companies that are joining securities markets to float IPO. Due to stringent entry rules that require them to be sound enough to be listed, they are usually fast-growing entities requiring more capital for expansion. Thus, they experience more interest from both traders and investors than those entities that have been old enough in the securities market.

Why IPOs for Swing trading consideration

New companies are untested. Most have experienced fast-growth and positive news in the market before deciding to go for a public listing. Thus, there is usually overwhelming interest, prospects, and speculations. This creates significant swings. Also, due to relatively huge volumes being floated at a go, they also attract the interest of large-scale traders and investors, which helps to pour more vitriol to their volatility. Swing traders find this a lucrative opportunity to dive into.

Why are IPOs so profitable to swing traders

As we have discussed, most IPOs experience rather vigorous swings. The higher the swing the higher the profit margin for a swing trader. This, accompanied by a huge volume of offload, means gross profit is only limited to your financial capacity.

How do you find IPOs?

The best way to find IPOs is to have an ear on the ground. Listen to financial news often. Closely follow financial social media. Identify successful startups that are experiencing rapid growth and keep abreast on information oozing from them, even if it is coming from its vineyard.

IPO investment strategy - mistakes to avoid

- Losing the opportunity to take profits – IPOs, though they rise most of the time, are unpredictable in the first few days. Have a good selling (exit) strategy. Unnecessary delays can cause you losses. Reap your profits shortly after listing days, once you have achieved your profit targets. Unless you are in for a long-term investment, cash in your gains when a chance presents itself. You can always buy back later once you are comfortable with the trend of the stock

- Rushing for IPO stocks on the first trading day – Unless you have strong faith in the IPO's potential, it is always prudent to wait for a few days for the stock to clear its pattern before you begin to buy more. Generally, IPOs normally trade higher than their offering price when listed. However, they succumb to profit taking a few days later. You can profit from them once they recover from the first correction and starts rallying.

- Succumbing to publicity and hypes – IPOs are usually heavily promoted by underwriters, no matter how unattractive the investment offer could be. Thus, it is prudent not to invest your emotions on these hypes.

- Trusting brokers on IPO – Brokers want to sell IPOs for lucrative gains from underwriters. This could push them hard and thus put self-interest first.

- Avoid being trapped by brand marketing – IPOs with familiar brand names are more often than not, overvalued and sometimes over-floated. This may cause them not to pick up once listed. It is not rare to find popular brand names without strong financial backing, which means its fundamentals are poor.

- Lack of stop-loss plan – Investing without a stop-loss is risking your investment IPOs often appeal to emotions. This could give you too much confidence such that you overlook risks involved. Make sure that your IPO investment is backed by a stop-loss.

Flipping

Flipping refers to buying and selling IPOs immediately the market opens in order to realize quick profits.

Why flip?

The intent is to buy low, sell high and exit with a quick profit. Thus, an IPO flipper buys an allotment of shares in the primary market of a company going public and then sells them right away in the secondary market instead of holding onto them. This is because, the IPO price is often lower than the open price, thus allowing one to make a quick profit. On the other hand, IPOs are highly volatile. They can easily plummet within a short time.

BEARISH MARKETS

Bears flourish in bearish markets. This is their territory. This is where they find conducive living conditions.

What is a 'Bear Market'?

This is a condition in which securities prices experience an overall downward trend. This breeds market pessimism, which causes the market's self-sustained downward spiral. In this condition, investors anticipate losses and thus rush to offload their investments to cut down on these losses. Generally, a downward of 20% in broad market indexes over a two-month period is deemed as an entry into a bear market.

Characteristics of a bear market

A bear market lasts for several quarters to a few years. Average bear markets last for about 3 years. Most new entrants to stock trading often confuse a correction and a bear market. A correction is a short-term trend lasting for less than two months. Corrections offer a good time for bullish traders to find an entry pot. On the other hand, a bear market hardly provides a suitable entry point for bullish traders as it is impossible to determine a bear market's bottom.

Short selling in a bear market

Short selling is a technique that involves selling borrowed shares and buying them back at lower prices to return to the lender (stockbroker).

Bullish vs. Bearish

In a bullish market, traders generally acquire stocks from an initial outbreak; hold them as they check out for profit targets on the upward trend.

In a bullish market, traders do not have this luxury of easy profits. Trends survive for short duration of time. Markets easily consolidate while prices keep on swinging and markets follow them in some sideways directions. There is no joyriding on a trend.

Bullish swing vs. Bearish swing

A bullish swing is characterized by higher highs and higher lows in an uptrend. By connecting these higher highs and higher lows together, a bullish channel can be established. You can use a 50-period simple moving average to identify the trend. If the moving average is going upwards and price action is above the moving average, that is a confirmed bullish swing (confirmed uptrend).

A bearish swing is characterized by lower highs and lower lows in a downtrend. By connecting these lower highs and lower lows together, a bearish channel can be established. The 50-period moving average goes downwards and price action moves below the moving average to confirm a bearish swing (bear trend/downtrend).

Range trading in a bear market

While bullish market depends on trends, bear market depends more on ranges than trends. Thus, in a bearish market, range trading is less risky compared to trend trading.

Ways to Profit in a Bear Market

Making a profit in a bearish market is tricky, unlike making a profit in a bullish market. However, you can easily find better chances of making huge profits in the bearish market as most bullish herds run away from it, thus leaving you with plenty of space and tons of opportunities. It is all about you mastering the skills of a successful hunting bear.

The following are some of the ways to profit in a bear market.

1. Find a good stock to buy – Go for a stock with higher earning potential
2. Hunt for dividends – A dividend is an extra benefit to gain in addition to reaping from price swings.

3. Watch out for bond rating - A company with a good bond rating has good returns and less risky. Watch out for companies with AAA rating.

4. Switch sectors according to economic performance – When the economy is doing well, companies dealing with luxuries make good returns. Their shares become profitable. On the other hand, when the economy is doing badly, you have to escape them. Instead, invest in stocks of companies dealing with necessities, as people will still need to consume them. Exchange-traded Funds (ETFs) are good vehicles for making this sector-wide move.

5. Go short on bad stocks – Bad stocks plunge deeper than good stocks. Thus, they are the most ideal for bearish traders.

6. Use margin cleverly – A margin is a soft loan advanced by a stockbroker for you to buy stocks. The best trick is to use margin on dividend-paying stocks immediately after they have corrected.

7. Purchase a call option – A call option a contract that gives the buyer the right to by a particular security within a specified period at a specified price. This option is based on the expectation that the security fetches a higher price

within a short duration. This needs proper timing. The best time to buy is when the bear market is about to hit the floor so that you can gain during its rise.

8. Use a covered call – This means that you are hedge a call option using your own stock. In essence, you undertake a commitment to sell your security to the call's holder (buyer) at an agreed price should the security rise to meet or exceed the strike price. In consideration of your undertaking, you receive an option premium (income on call). This is a less risky option compared to a normal call option.

9. Use a put option to realize earnings – This option commits you to buy a certain amount of shares (usually 100) at a specified price within the relevant option period. A put option entitles you to a premium (income). Since you are interested in buying the stock when the price falls (to reimburse the lender), you benefit more since you are being rewarded for it.

10. Patiently wait to strike good income – While a bearish market can take long, it can be highly rewarding. Thus, the more patient you are, the more likely you are going to hit it big. However, this is more of investing than trading.

EARNINGS ANNOUNCEMENTS DRIFT

Ultimately, every investor desires a reward for his/her investment. Equities too have their own returns. Companies declare earnings on a periodic basis - quarterly, semi-annually or annually. These earnings inform investors of the performance of their investments in terms of shares.

More often than not, earnings announcements cause a reaction in the market. This reaction causes a drift in the share price, either upwards or downwards, depending on potential earnings.

As a swing trader, you are interested in reaping profit from this drift in share price.

There are two main types of Earnings Announcement Drift:

1. Pre-earnings announcement drift
2. PEAD

Pre-earnings announcement drift

Most companies have a policy of declaring earnings at certain specific calendar dates. Surplus or demand may rise in the market due to speculative causes prior to the earnings announcement. This is what is called Pre-earnings announcement drift.

However, pre-earning announcement drift is not such pronounced as the post-earnings announcement drift, unless triggered by serious rumors or signals in the market.

PEAD

PEAD is an acronym for Post-earnings Announcement Drift. This refers to the peculiar response of stocks to the earnings announcement, which causes them to trigger cumulative abnormal returns drift lasting weeks to months in the direction of the earnings surprise.

Why is PEAD important for Swing traders?

Swing traders are simply interested in profit margin. PEAD provides an opportunity for a swing. This swing could be high or low depending on the impact of earnings on the share value. The swing could be upward or downward.

If the announcement is about positive earnings, then, the swing is more likely going to be upwards. However, if the announcement declares negative earnings, then, the swing is more likely to be downwards. However, the ultimate behavior will depend on how far and how much the declared earnings deviate from the previous periods.

For example, if the previous period earning per share (EPS) was $1.2 and the current EPS is $0.7, then, although the EPS is positive, it is still negative in relation to the previous period. This may not necessarily trigger a serious upward swing. Instead, it could end up triggering a downward swing. On the other hand, if the previous EPS was $0.7 and the current EPS is $1.2 then; this will naturally trigger an upward swing since it shows a positive trend.

Similarly, if the announcement declares negative earnings, then the swing is more likely going to be downwards. However, if the previous EPS was -$0.6 and the current EPS is -0.1, then, there is more likely going to be an upward swing since there is a positive trend. On the other hand, if the previous EPS was -$0.1 and the current EPS is -$6, then, naturally, there will be a downward swing since the trend is negative.

In both upswing and downswing, a swing trader can take action depending on whether he is a bullish swing trader or a bearish swing trader.

What you need to know about PEAD

PEAD is more pronounced in:

- Thinly traded stocks
- Stocks with analyst coverage
- Stocks with revenue surprise in addition to earnings surprise

PEAD Returns can persist even beyond a quarter

Characteristics to look for to identify the best PEAD

Look for extreme:

- Earnings growth (early stages of growth)
- Sales growth (early stages of growth with a potential to explode beyond a billion-dollar mark)
- Price strength (starting young trend characterized by an explosive first leg)
- Neglect (low float and low volume for many years)

PEAD Strategy

This strategy aims at skimming off profits from the earning surprise (ES). ES is the difference between earnings estimates and reported earnings.

Basic strategy:

- Sell securities with ES in the bottom decile.
- Buy securities with ES in the upper decile

Relatively advanced strategy:

In addition to simple PEAD strategy, factor in recency ratio. Thus;

- Sell securities with most extremely negative ES (bottom decile) and low recency ratio (bottom 1:3).
- buy securities with most extremely positive ES (upper decile) and high recency ration (top 1:3)

Which Stocks Will Enjoy a PEAD?

To predict stocks likely to enjoy a PEAD, check for earnings release that fulfills the following three things:

- A sales surprise
- An earnings surprise
- Company-based raised future earnings estimates

BEARISH SETUPS

To be able to reap maximum profits from trend following, it is imperative that you can establish setups.

What is a setup?

For securities trading, a setup refers to a combination of various factors that gives us the right perspective about the future direction of a stock's price. These factors include price signals, price pattern, and technical indicators. These setups are well-established using charting tools. However, we must not forget that these setups do not reflect exact events in the future. They are simply predictive and thus based on a high probability of occurrence. In essence, they are high-probability setups.

To be able to set appropriate setups, you have to establish rules guiding these setups to guide your decision-making.

Bearish setups

Bearish setups are those setups based on a bearish perspective. The following are the three main types of bearish setups:

1. The Relief Rally

2. The Bearish Divergence

3. The Blue Sea Breakdown

These are identified based on three key factors:

- Market type

- Characteristics

- Key indicators

The Relief Rally

Market type:

Both strongly trending and weakly trending bearish markets

Characteristics:

- A stock that is strongly or weakly down trending, but has rallied up beyond its lows to reach a major moving average, which acts as a resistance.
- Entry decision is based on confirmation of an overbought condition as evidenced by the stochastic indicator and a confirmation by a bearish candlestick.
- Likely triggered by a response to news announcements, a short squeeze (shorts forced to cover their positions and

buyback due to a surprise reversal) or a spate of short-term profit-taking.

Key indicators:

Strong or weakly down trending stock that has rallied up into a downward sloping 50 MA (weakly down trending) or 20 MA (strongly down trending).

1. Sharp rise in stochastic (five-period) to or over the overbought 80 line.
2. Bearish candle of some kind (put in by price on the rally to that moving average).
3. All these three factors register a short sell signal, which indicates that the stock is ready to be registered as a valid relief rally setup.

The Bearish Divergence

Market type:

Weakly trending bearish markets and Range-bound markets

Characteristics:

- Stock that is trading within a long-range downtrend, but which is currently in a substantial rally and has registered a series of higher heights

- Pinpoints the tops of sharp rallies, that is, beyond 50 MA within long-range downtrends.

- At least two heights long are required for basis of comparison. Yet, not too many.

Key indicators:

- Stock being in a long-range
- Above 50 MA. At least two clear price highs. The last price high corresponds with a lower high in two or more of key indicator tools: Stochastic, MACD histogram, RSI, MACD, CCI, or OBV.

If the last price high corresponds to a prior price resistance, trendline resistance or 200 MA, the better is the indicator.

A sell short signal is triggered when a bearish candle is printed on the daily chart once the above key indicators have been met.

The Blue Sea Breakdown

Market type:

Strongly trending bearish markets

Characteristics:

A reverse cup and handle formation. It is the opposite of Blue Sea. A Blue Sea is a new low territory that a stock trades down into as clears (at least 3 months) of prior price lows.

Key indicators:

- The closing price of the stock must register a new low immediately following a previous new low set within the past twenty trading days. This new low must be a consequence of a recent and short-lived move in price as opposed to a persistent sell-off.

- The current new closing price low must be a significant low, that is, a new low closing price low must be registered within at least the past three months of trading.

- The new closing price low must not have a run far below the 52-week high for the particular stock. Thus, the stock must not be too overextended to the downside.

- The current breakdown into Blue Sea territory (that is, no price support within the last previous three months) must be accompanied by the lowest OBV reading witnessed in at least the past three months.

- The candle on the day of breakdown to a new low must be a red candle (that is, the close must be lower than the open).

When all these indicators have been met on the same day, this makes up a sell short signal.

CONCLUSION

Thank for acquiring and reading this book 'Swing Trading: A Beginners Guide to Making Money With Trend Following'

I hope the information provided in this book has enabled you to learn Swing. It is also my sincere hope that you have been inspired enough to start trading in equity stocks. If you found this book to be helpful, kindly share information about it with others and encourage them to acquire a copy so that they took can benefit.

Have a good luck!

www.ingramcontent.com/pod-product-compliance
Lightning Source LLC
Chambersburg PA
CBHW071514210326
41597CB00018B/2752